# THE
# FASTEST
## AND
# SLOWEST

First edition for the United States, Canada,
and the Philippines published 1992
by Barron's Educational Series, Inc.

© Copyright by Aladdin Books Ltd 1992

Design  David West Children's Book Design
Illustrator  David West
Text Anita Ganeri
Picture research  Emma Krikler

Created and designed by
N.W. Books
28 Percy Street
London W1P 9FF

All inquiries should be addressed to:
Barron's Educational Series, Inc.
250 Wireless Boulevard
Hauppauge, NY 11788

International Standard Book No. 0-8120-6290-6

Library of Congress Catalog Card No. 92-10077

**Library of Congress Cataloging-in-Publication Data**

Ganeri, Anita. 1961 -
The fastest and slowest / Anita Ganeri ; [illustrator, David
West]. -- 1st ed. for the U.S., Canada, and the Philippines.
p.  cm. -- (Questions and answers about--)
Summary: Cartoons and color photographs accompany answers to
questions about some of the fastest or slowest record breakers.
ISBN 0-8120-6290-6
1. World records--Miscellanea--Juvenile literature. 2. Children's
questions and answers.  [1. World records--Miscellanea.
2. Questions and answers.] I. West, David, ill. II. Title.
III. Series: Ganeri, Anita, 1961- Questions and answers about-- .
AG243.G28  1992
031.02--dc20          92-10077          CIP          AC
Printed in Belgium
234  987654321

# QUESTIONS AND ANSWERS ABOUT

## THE
# FASTEST
## AND
# SLOWEST

## Barron's

## The Fastest and Slowest

The USA's Lockheed SR-71 is the world's fastest jet plane. It has flown at a speed of 2,206 miles (3,530 kilometers) an hour, nearly four times faster than a jumbo jet. This book will help you to learn about some of the fastest and slowest record breakers. They include plants and animals, cars and trains, and planets.

# Which fish swims the fastest?

The sailfish is the fastest fish in the sea. It can speed along at nearly 68 miles (110 kilometers) an hour. This is faster than a cheetah. The sailfish has a torpedo-shaped body. It can also fold its back fin down into its body as it swims. These features make it streamlined for speed.

**Which is the fastest animal on land?**
Cheetahs can sprint along at 62 miles (100 kilometers) an hour as they chase after zebras and gazelles. This is faster than a galloping racehorse. The cheetah is the fastest mover on land.

## Which plants grow the fastest?

Some types of bamboo can grow up to 36 inches (91 centimeters) a day. If you grew at this rate, you would be over 10 miles (16 kilometers) tall by the time you were five years old. This is nearly twice as high as Mount Everest! The giant kelp of the Pacific Ocean can grow 18 inches (45 centimeters) a day. But a strand of this seaweed never grows longer than about 210 feet (65 meters).

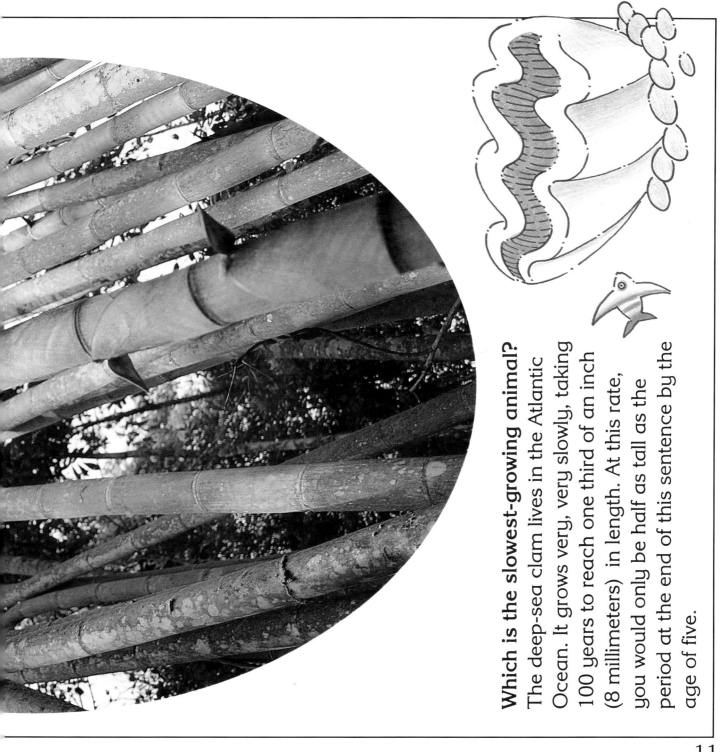

## Which is the slowest-growing animal?

The deep-sea clam lives in the Atlantic Ocean. It grows very, very slowly, taking 100 years to reach one third of an inch (8 millimeters) in length. At this rate, you would only be half as tall as the period at the end of this sentence by the age of five.

11

## What was the fastest speed reached in space?

In 1969, three astronauts flew at a speed of 24,792 miles (39,897 kilometers) an hour. They were part of the Apollo 10 space mission. This is the fastest speed at which people have ever traveled. At this speed, it would take just over an hour to go right around Earth at the equator.

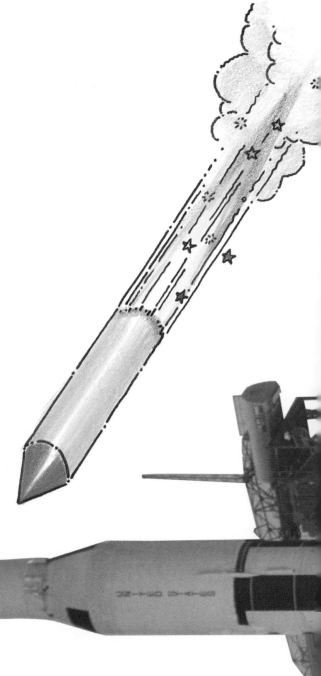

## Which were the slowest rockets?

The first war rockets were made in China about 950 years ago. They were fired at enemy horses to scare them. The rockets were powered by gunpowder. They could not travel very fast at all – probably no faster than you could throw one!

# Which is the fastest-spinning planet?

Earth takes about 24 hours to spin around once on its axis. But Jupiter takes just 9 hours, 50 minutes and 30 seconds. This makes it the fastest-spinning planet in our solar system. If you stood on Earth's equator, you would be traveling at a speed of 325 miles (523 kilometers) an hour. On Jupiter's equator, you would be traveling at an amazing 28,270 miles (45,500 kilometers) an hour!

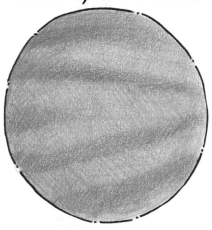

**Which planet spins the slowest?**
Venus is the slowest-spinning planet. It takes 243 days to turn around once on its axis. In this time, Jupiter would have spun over 580 times.

# Which is the fastest car?

Thrust 2 is the fastest car that has ever run. In 1983, Richard Noble drove it over the Black Rock Desert in Nevada. The car reached a speed of 634 miles (1,019 kilometers) an hour, the fastest ever on land. Thrust 2 uses special jet engines, like those in an airplane.

## Which was the slowest car?

One of the first cars to carry passengers was built in France in 1769. It was a type of steam-driven tractor. Its top speed was just 2¼ miles (3.6 kilometers) an hour. This is about as fast as you walk.

# Which jet plane can fly the slowest?

The Harrier "jump-jet" can fly at 0 miles (kilometers) an hour - it hovers! It has two rotating exhaust nozzles on each side of its body. When the nozzles point downward the plane rises in a vertical take-off. The nozzles are then angled backward to propel the plane forward.

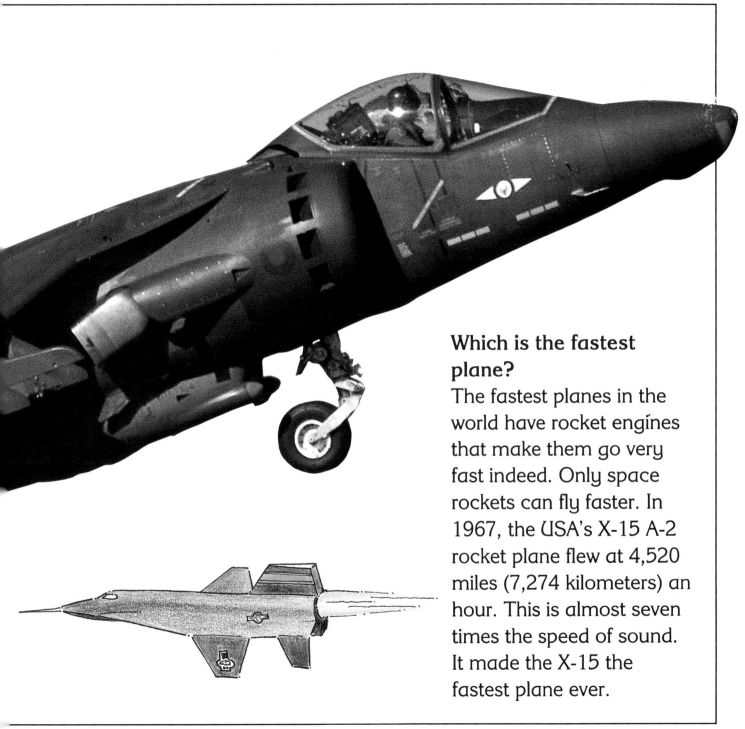

## Which is the fastest plane?

The fastest planes in the world have rocket engines that make them go very fast indeed. Only space rockets can fly faster. In 1967, the USA's X-15 A-2 rocket plane flew at 4,520 miles (7,274 kilometers) an hour. This is almost seven times the speed of sound. It made the X-15 the fastest plane ever.

# Which is the fastest train?

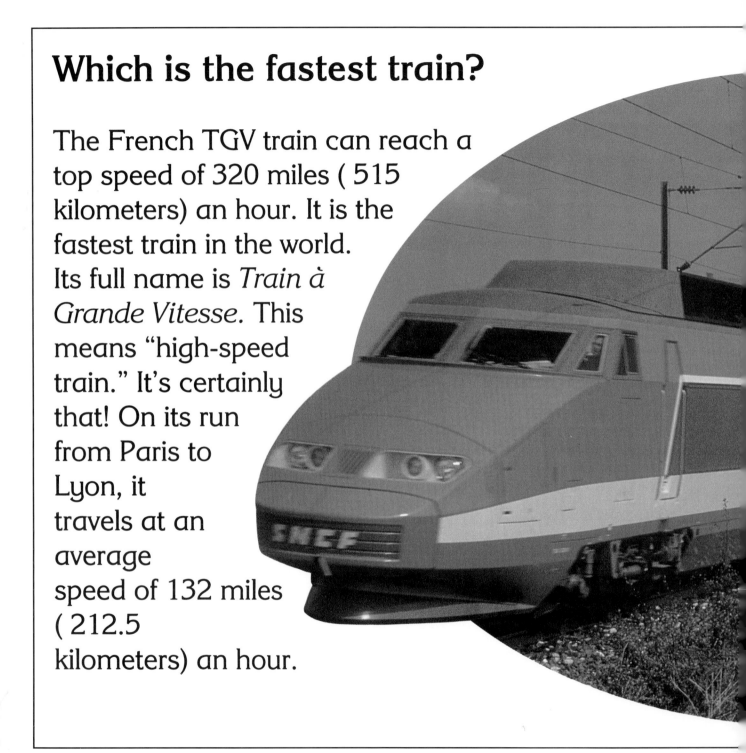

The French TGV train can reach a top speed of 320 miles ( 515 kilometers) an hour. It is the fastest train in the world. Its full name is *Train à Grande Vitesse.* This means "high-speed train." It's certainly that! On its run from Paris to Lyon, it travels at an average speed of 132 miles ( 212.5 kilometers) an hour.

## Which trains ran the slowest?

The first steam-powered train ran much more slowly than trains today. The first public railroad opened in 1825. Steam trains carried passengers between Stockton and Darlington in England. They chugged along at 15 miles (24 kilometers) an hour.

# What was the fastest crossing of the Atlantic Ocean?

Sea Cat is a type of boat known as a catamaran. It was launched in January 1990. In June 1990, it crossed the Atlantic Ocean at an average speed of 46 miles (74 kilometers) an hour. This set a new record for the fastest crossing. Sea Cat is now being used to carry passengers between England and France.

**What is the fastest speed ever on water?**
In 1977, Kenneth Warby reached the highest speed ever on water. He drove his seaplane, Spirit of Australia, at 346 miles (556 kilometers) an hour over a lake in Australia. This is nearly twice the top speed of a racing car.

# How fast did the fastest wind blow?

Winds that blow at speeds of over 74 miles (119 kilometers) an hour are called hurricanes. They can damage buildings, pull trees up and destroy farmers' crops. But the fastest wind ever blew almost four times faster than this. It was a tornado that happened in Texas in 1958. It reached a speed of 280 miles (450 kilometers) an hour.

## Where do the fastest floods happen?

Deserts are usually very dry places. But it sometimes rains so heavily that it causes floods. These are called flash floods because they happen so quickly. In 1972, there was a flash flood in Calama, Chile. This desert town had had no rain for 400 years!

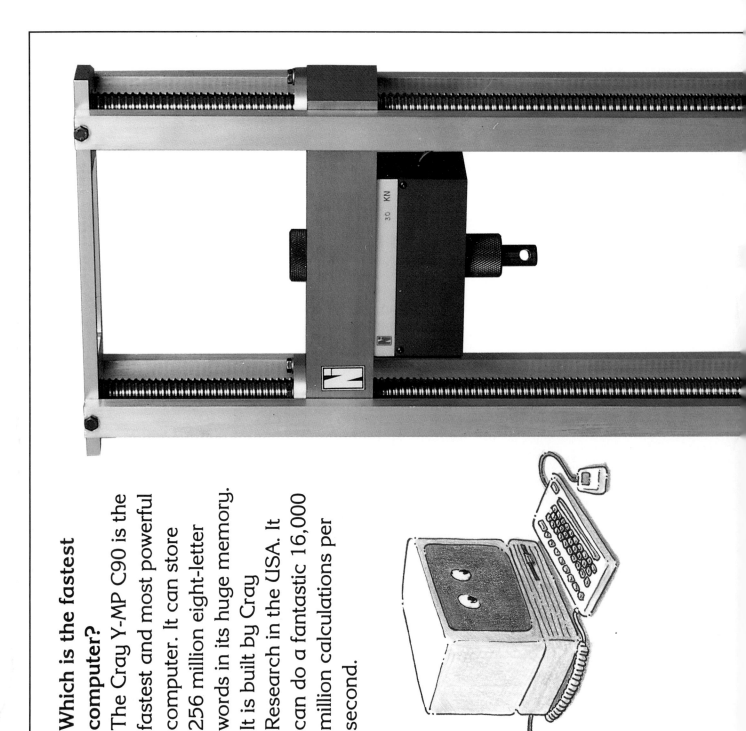

## Which is the fastest computer?

The Cray Y-MP C90 is the fastest and most powerful computer. It can store 256 million eight-letter words in its huge memory. It is built by Cray Research in the USA. It can do a fantastic 16,000 million calculations per second.

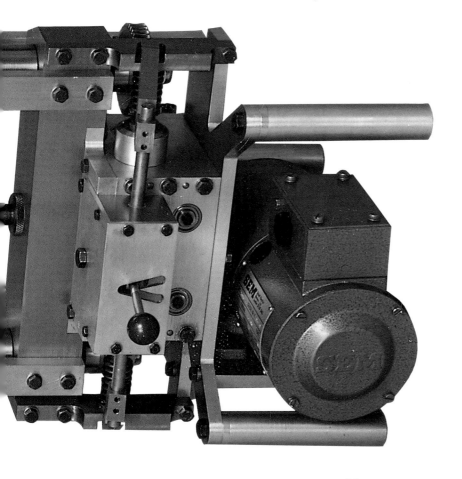

## Which is the slowest machine?

The slowest machine in the world is used to test the strength of metal objects, such as ships' propellers. It can be remotely controlled at very, very low speeds. Its slowest working speed is one million millionth of a millimeter a minute. At this speed, it would take an ant about a billion years to walk right across these two pages.

27

# What is the fastest thing ever?

Light is the fastest thing we know of. It travels at 186,000 miles (300,000 kilometers) a second. A rocket traveling at this speed would reach the Moon in just over a second. Distances in space are so huge that they are measured in light years. A light year is the distance that light travels in one year, which is nearly 6 trillion miles (9.5 trillion kilometers).

## What is the fastest piece of music?

*The Flight of the Bumble Bee* is one of the fastest pieces of music. It was written by the composer Rimsky-Korsakov in 1899, and was intended for musicians to show off their skill by playing as fast as possible. It was part of an opera about a prince who turns into a bumblebee to sting his villainous aunts.

# Index

**Photographs**

Cover and page 16-17: Richard and Sally Noble; title page 18-19: Paul Nightingale; pages 6-7 and 15: Frank Spooner Pictures; pages 8-9, 10-11 and 28-29: Planet Earth Pictures; page 12-13: NASA; page 20-21: Topham Picture Source; page 23: Hoverpseed; page 24-25: Science Photo Library; page 26-27: Nene Instruments.